S[illegible] p[illegible] your man

• BECCA THOMPSON •

BOATSWAIN PRESS
EMSWORTH

Introduction

This book has been designed for those men who always say 'I'd like to get fit' but don't know how to start. It provides a series of safe effective exercises progressed in logical sequence that can be carried out at any time of day in the house or office! Ideally they should be performed 3 times a week and to really see and feel the benefits should be combined with aerobic exercise for the heart and lungs such as walking, jogging, swimming or cycling.

The benefits of getting and staying fit are well known but to recap you will look and feel in better shape, be more able to cope with the stresses and strains of everyday life and according to research enjoy a better sex life. What more convincing do you need?

The results achieved depend very much on how hard, how long and how often you are prepared to exercise. If performed regularly the exercises in this book will help you see and feel improvements in the shape and tone of your body.

Are you fit enough?

Exercise is the key to a fit and healthy body. However, it does not suit everyone and some people can be adversely affected by exercise. Ask yourself some simple questions before trying these exercises. If the answer is 'yes' to *one or more* of the questions below consult your doctor. Answer 'no' to the questions and you are ready to start. So have fun and think of the improvements you are making.

Questions

- Has your doctor ever advised you that you have heart trouble or is there a history of heart disease in your family?
- Do you often have pains in your heart or chest?
- Do you have dizzy spells, headaches or suffer from fainting?
- Do you have problems with any joints, especially those that have been aggravated by exercise?
- Are your presently taking any medication?
- Do you have any other medical condition which makes you think you may not be able to exercise? If you are at all unsure check with your doctor first.

Safety

It is very important to prepare the body and mind for strenuous exercise. It is often very tempting to plough straight into the toning exercises without giving due consideration to your body's mechanics.

Incorporated in this book are '*Warm up*' exercises to mobilise the joints and stretches to prepare the muscles – warm muscles work more effectively and prevent injury. It is essential to allow the heart and lungs time to gradually accustomise to more strenous activity. It is important that the body must be given time to recover after exercising, and the '*Cooldown*' section suggests stretches for the specific muscle groups used. These enable the muscles to be stretched comfortably to a pre-exercise state and prevent soreness and stiffness the following day.

So always remember to Warm up and Cooldown.

Never exercise on a full stomach. Don't eat or drink *(except water)* when exercising. Having started, maintain the continuity and after the warm up go straight on to the toning exercise or aerobic activity *(if you have time).* Do not stop for lunch or a tea break in between. Some of the exercises within the toning section show alternatives using a chair. Be very careful to ensure that the furniture you use is quite stable.

Always *STOP* if any exercise or stretch hurts. Recheck your exercise position against the diagram or try an alternative exercise working the same muscle group. If you still feel uncomfortable then please *STOP*. Don't force stretch positions, never bounce or hold a stretch for too long. If you are unused to regular exercise it may take a while to become comfortable so only hold for 6/8 seconds and build up gradually. It is essential not to overdo things in the beginning. The best results will be achieved by a slow, gradual build up of exercises carried out on a regular basis.

Posture check

Think about your posture and your body alignment. This applies in everyday life as well as during exercise! Stand tall with your feet 'hip' width apart and tilt the pelvis forward slightly pulling the stomach in and tucking your bottom under. Raise the shoulders up, push them back and drop them down, keeping them relaxed. The back should be straight and head high. Remember, keep the knees slightly bent, *never* lock out the joints. This *'posture check'* is referred to throughout the book, so make sure you master it.

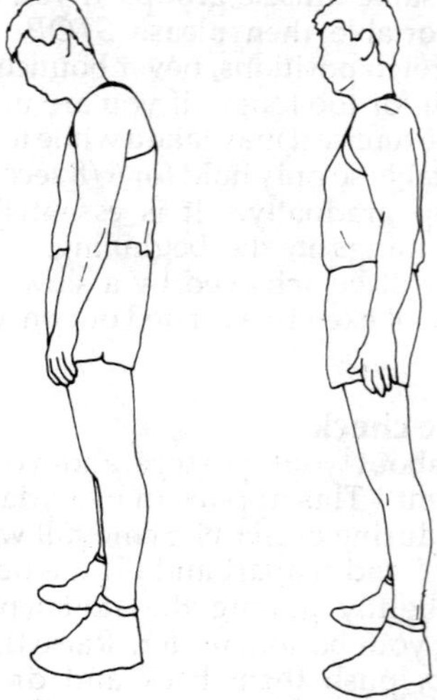

Warm up

It is essential to prepare the body and mind for exercise. By warming up before the more strenuous exercises in the toning section you will prevent injury and soreness in the muscles and joints and achieve greater results from your exercises. The warm up is broken down into three parts – mobility, pulse raising and stretches.

MOBILITY exercises will 'loosen up' the joints by performing the exercise through a full range of movement to stimulate fluid in the joint which will improve exercise technique and help prevent injury.

PULSE RAISING exercises such as swing steps and knee lifts gradually increase the body temperature and allow time for the extra blood supply to reach the working muscles. This gradual build up in exercising allows time for the heart and lungs to accustomise to the more strenous exercises to come during the toning section. Finally, when the muscles are a little warmer, we perform a few *STRETCHES*, each held for approximately 8 seconds, to prepare the muscles, help prevent injury and allow for improved movement quality.

Before starting ensure you have read and answered *Are you fit enough to exercise?* on page 3. Also make sure you have enough room to exercise comfortably – preferably on a carpeted area or using a towel or mat as a base – and perhaps play some cheerful, stimulating music to help you exercise. It is also important to wear loose comfortable clothing that won't restrict your movements. If you are exercising in the office remember to remove your tie! This warm up is designed to help you attain the maximum benefits safely from your toning exercises and therefore achieve the best results.

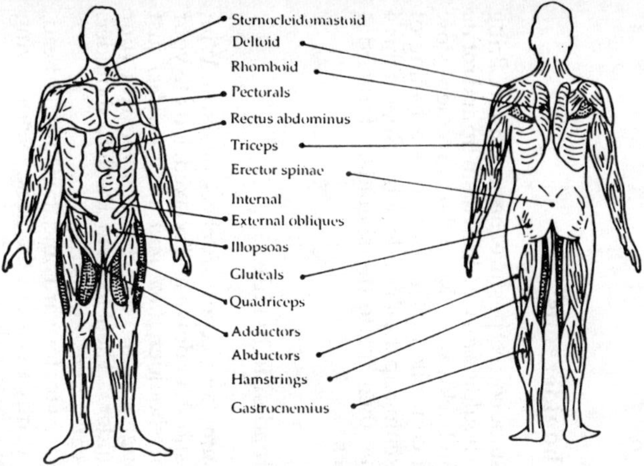

Sternocleidomastoid
Deltoid
Rhomboid
Pectorals
Rectus abdominus
Triceps
Erector spinae
Internal
External obliques
Illopsoas
Gluteals
Quadriceps
Adductors
Abductors
Hamstrings
Gastrocnemius

WARM UP EXERCISES

1 Shoulder rolls

Assume correct posture check position. Bring the shoulders forward, lift them up and rotate them backwards. Keep the movement slow and controlled. This promotes a feeling of loosening up the shoulder joint. Repeat this 4 times then rotate the shoulders forward 4 times.

2 Head side to side

Assume correct posture check position. With the shoulder down and relaxed, look to your right shoulder, *(not over the shoulder)* just enough so that your chin is level with your shoulder. Then look to the left shoulder. Repeat 4 times each side.
Always face forwards and then turn the head, this gently eases out the neck. *Never* swing from side to side.

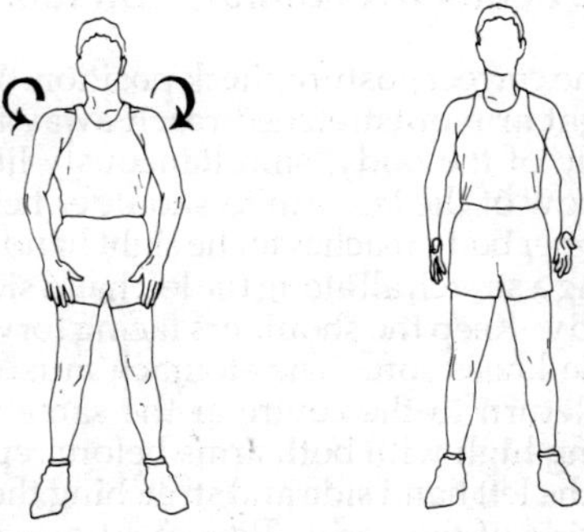

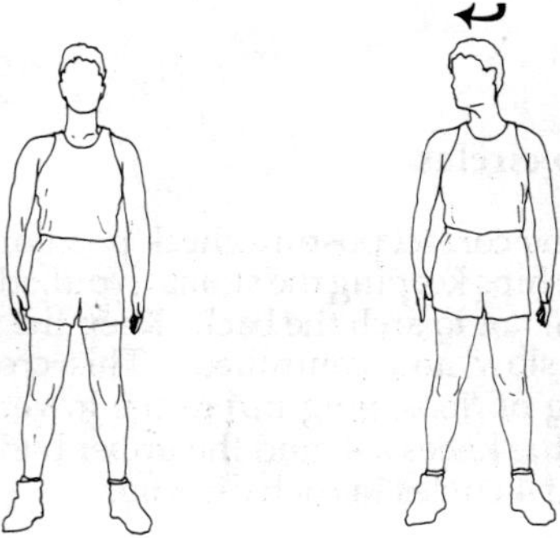

3 Side bends with double arm raise

Assume correct posture check position. With the right arm outstretched reach away from the side of the body, simultaneously lifting the elbow of the left arm to shoulder height. The upper body reaches to the right hand side creating a stretch all along the left hand side of the body. Keep the shoulders facing forward and the knees soft. The stomach must stay flat. Return to the centre at the same time reaching high with both arms before repeating to the left hand side and stretching the left hand side of the body. Repeat 4 times each side.

4 Hip circles

Assume correct posture check position. Circle the hips keeping the stomach pulled in. Be careful not to arch the back. Keep the movement slow and controlled. This creates a feeling of 'loosening up' in the lower back. Keep the knees soft and the upper body still. Repeat 4 circles in each direction.

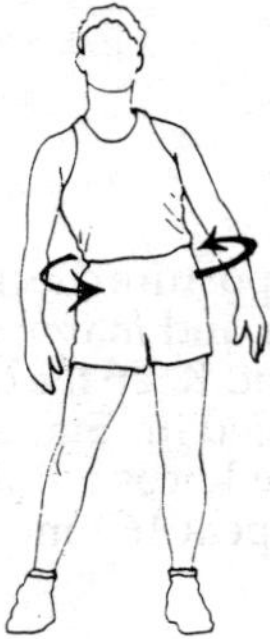

5 Knee bends

Place the feet a good distance apart, turned out slightly at 45 degrees. Keeping the stomach pulled in, the back straight and pelvis tilted forwards, bend and straighten the legs. Be sure not to lock out the knees as you come up. The knees go out over the toes and do not face forward. Do not bend too far as this is only a warm up exercise. Repeat 8 times. Then repeat 8 times adding the arms reaching down and pulling the elbows up to chest height as you extend the legs.

6 Marches

Assume correct posture check position. Bring the feet together and march on the spot. Do not stamp the feet. Keep the back straight and the stomach pulled in. Stand tall. Swing the arms and lift the knees a little higher to add some effort. Repeat 16 times.

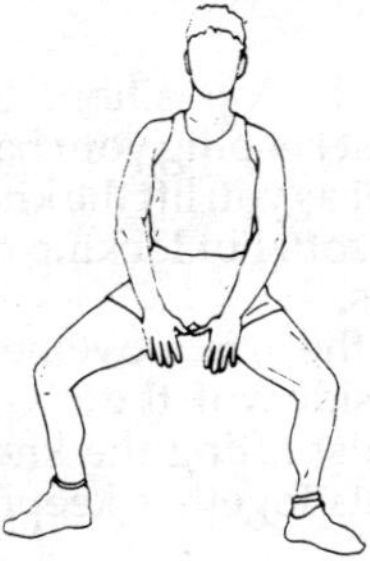

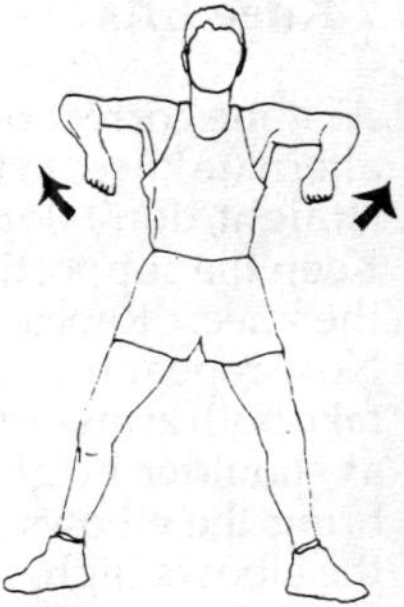

7 Knee lifts

Assume correct posture check position. Lift alternate knees to the chest keeping your back straight, don't slouch over as you lift the knee. Keep the supporting leg soft, not locking out the knee. Repeat 8 times.
Now repeat this adding the arm movement, take both arms out to the side with the elbows at shoulder height. Whilst lifting the knees bring the elbows and fists together keeping the elbows high.
If you find exercises 6 & 7 confusing using arm and leg movements leave out the arm movements until you are more familiar with the exercises.

8 Swing step

Take the feet wide apart and step from one foot to the other. Bend the knees through the middle as you transfer your weight. At the same time swing the arms at shoulder height. The more effort you put into this exercise by taking larger steps and bending more in the middle, the warmer you become. Repeat for 8 swings.

9 Swing step & heel raise

Repeat previous exercise, at the same time lift alternate heels in towards the bottom, making sure your supporting leg is always bent. Don't lock out the knees. Make sure you really bend the legs and exaggerate the arms to warm up. Repeat 8 times.

10 Jogging

Jog on the spot with the arms bent and moving freely beside you. Make sure you use a heel strike using the whole foot not just running on the ball of the foot. Every 8 counts (2 steps = 1 count) change direction to your right until you have completed a square (32 counts). If you already feel quite warm then substitute this exercise for marching on the spot. If, however, you are not yet warm please repeat exercises 8-10 before stretching and starting the toning exercises.

WARM UP STRETCHES

11 Front thigh stretch

Quadricep

Assume correct posture check position. Bend the left supporting leg slightly and draw the opposite heel in towards the bottom holding the foot near the ankle *(not curling the toes)*. Keep the hips square and pushed forward and the knees together. Feel the stretch in the front of the right thigh. Do not lock out the knee of the supporting leg. Hold for 6-8 seconds. Repeat both sides.

12 Calf stretch

Gastrocnemius

Assume correct posture check position. Place one heel behind you. The front knee is bent, knee is over the ankle and rear leg is straight. Push through the rear heel to the floor. Keep the hips and shoulders square and check that the rear toe is facing forward not out to the side. Feel the stretch in the top of the calf muscle in the straight leg. Hold for 6-8 seconds, repeat on the other leg.

13 Lunge

Adductors

Assume correct posture check position. Take the feet a good distance apart turning the toes out slightly to 45 degrees. Bend the right knee, the knee should be in line with the ankle. This straightens the left leg. You should feel a comfortable stretch in the inner thigh. Keep the shoulder and hips square. Hold for 6-8 seconds, repeat other side.

14 Back of thigh stretch

Hamstring

Assume correct posture check position. Bend your left supporting leg slightly, place your right foot flat to the floor in front of the body, keeping the leg straight. Lean forwards slightly keeping the chest lifted and the stomach pulled in. Support yourself by placing your hands on the left thigh. Feel the stretch all behind the right thigh. To increase the stretch, flex the foot of the extended leg. Hold for 6-8 seconds, repeat other leg.

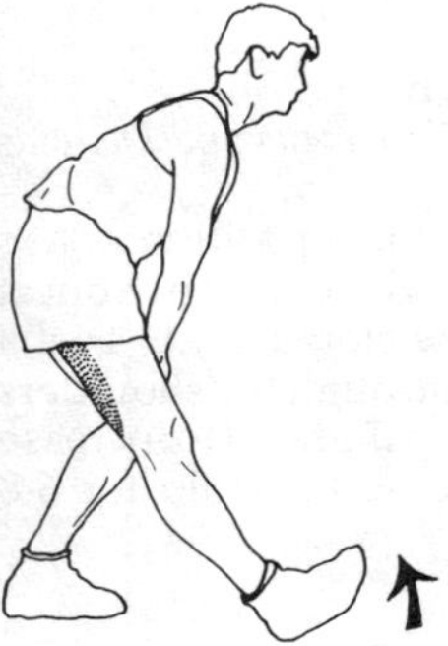

15 Side stretch

Latissimus dorsi & Obliques

Assume correct posture check position but with feet a little wider apart. Place one hand on your hip and take the other arm outstretched over the head. Feel a comfortable stretch all along the side of the body. Keep the shoulders and hips facing forward. Remember the knees should be slightly bent and the stomach pulled in. Breathe normally as you hold the stretch position. Hold for 6-8 seconds. Repeat other side.

16 Upper back stretch

Trapezius and Deltoids

Assume correct posture check position. Clasp hands together and extend the arms in front at chest height, pulling the stomach in. Feel a comfortable stretch all through the shoulders and the upper back. Drop the head to increase the stretch through the neck. Hold for 6-8 seconds.

17 Tricep stretch

Triceps

Assume correct posture check position. Place the right hand over your head with the finger tips between your shoulder blades. The left hand rests gently on the right elbow to ease the arm into position. If you feel uncomfortable in this position place the left arm on the right arm in front of the body rather than above as shown in the diagram. Hold for 6-8 seconds. Feel the stretch in the back of the upper arm. Repeat other side.

18 Chest stretch

Pectorals

Assume correct posture check position. Clasp your hands together behind you, squeeze the shoulder blades together as you lift the hands slightly away from the body. Be careful not to lock out the elbows or arch the back. Feel the stretch all across the chest. Hold for 6-8 seconds.

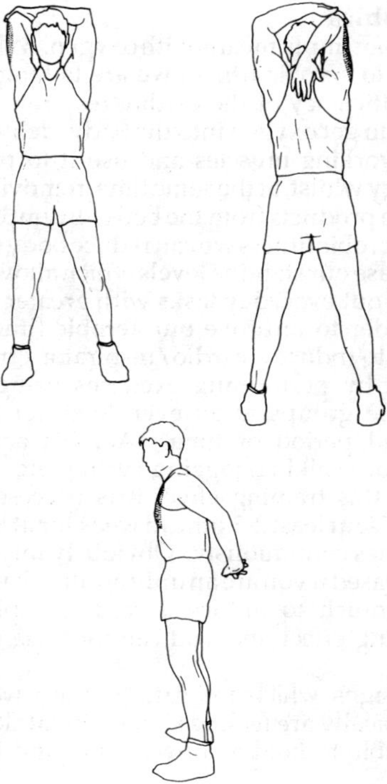

Aerobics

Aerobic simply means with oxygen. When we refer to aerobic fitness we are talking about the efficiency of the cardio/respiratory systems to get oxygen into the body, deliver it to the working muscles and use it to provide energy whilst, at the same time, removing any waste products from the body. By improving our aerobic fitness we can reduce body fat and increase our stamina levels which allows us to carry out everyday tasks with greater ease.

In order to improve our aerobic fitness we have to induce a cardio/respiratory training effect by performing exercises using large muscle groups at an even level for an extended period of time. Aerobic activities include walking, jogging cycling etc. To induce this training effect it is neccessary to exercise at least 2-3 times a week for at least 20 minutes continuously. Obviously this can be decreased if you are an unfit adult as it will not take much to induce a cardio/respiratory training effect and you can increase gradually.

The signs which indicate you are working aerobically are feeling slightly breathless but still able to hold a conversation and feeling warmer and looking a little pink. These signs do *not* include being bright red, soaked in sweat and totally gasping for breath! In fact by exercising too intensely there will not be enough oxygen for your body to burn fat to produce energy and you will very quickly tire and may experience pain through harmful waste products *(lactic acid)* being produced. This type of exercise is called *anaerobic* (without oxygen) and includes sprinting and other forms of sudden stop/start activities which are really only appropriate for fitter athletes who find this anaerobic work necessary for their training.

As you become fitter you can increase the intensity, time and frequency you exercise – from walking to jogging, from 20 to 30 minutes or from 2 to 3 times a week – or a combination of all these. But always remember to do the warm up first before jogging or cycling round the block! And be aware that you should only feel slightly breathless and not uncomfortably exhausted.

Your aerobic activities can be done in addition to the toning exercises or on alternate days. There are many ways to include aerobic activities into your daily life such as cycling or walking to work, getting off the bus a stop earlier on the way to or from work, using the stairs instead of the lift etc. Try to choose activities you like and find relaxing rather than letting exercise become a chore.

Here are some excellent exercises/sports which improve your aerobic fitness.

Walking

aerobic fitness • burning fat • toning the lower body • reducing stress • low impact

Walk briskly for at least 20 minutes continuously. You should feel warmer and a little breathless–a good indication is to feel warmer but still be able to hold a conversation.

Jogging

aerobic fitness • burning fat • toning the lower body • reducing stress

Rowing

aerobic fitness • strength in back, legs and arms • flexibility • reducing stress • low impact

Cycling
aerobic fitness • toning the lower body • burning fat • reducing stress

Swimming
aerobic fitness • burning fat • toning the upper/ lower body • reducing stress • low impact

All these activities require you to do the *warm up* and the *cooldown*. The *warm up* to help prepare the body and mind for more strenuous exercise and help prevent injury and afterwards the *cooldown* to return the body to a pre-exercising state and help lengthen the muscles to prevent injury and stiffness.

In the list of benefits some exercises are said to be low impact, which means no jumping, one foot is always in contact with the ground / base. Therefore there is less stress through the body and less joint injury.

Toning

Having completed the warm up, you are ready to do the toning exercises to increase the strength and endurance of specific muscle groups and improve their shape and tone.

Muscular *strength* and muscular *endurance* are 2 different elements of fitness but in this section we have combined them. Muscular *strength* incorporates a low number of repetitions of an exercise with high resistance, whereas muscular *endurance* incorporates a high number of repetitions of an exercise using a low resistance. To improve the shape and tone of these muscles we must achieve postitive overload – the muscle is put in a situation where it must work against greater stress than it is used to – you reach muscle fatigue *not pain*. This is done by increasing the frequency, intensity and duration of your exercises. Build up the intensity gradually, start with a low number of repetitions and when you can comfortably do 3 sets of 8 repetitions move on to the alternative (b) exercise which is progressive.

It is important to alternate the exercises between different muscle groups and not to overwork or tire just one muscle group. Choose (a) or (b) of an exercise – ***not both.***

Then move on to (a) or (b) of another exercise using a different muscle group. For example, press ups using Pectorals and Triceps followed by curl ups using the Rectus abdominus. Each diagram shows a shaded area which indicates where you should feel the benefit of the exercise or stretch. We are all different and this may vary slightly. However if you do not feel the exercise/stretch in the area shown in the diagram, check and possibly re-adjust your exercise position – a slight realignment of an arm or leg can alter the muscle group you are aiming to work.

Do these exercises at your own pace, take a brief rest between sets and stretch out if you want and *stop* if it hurts. Exercise should not hurt to be beneficial. Try an alternative exercise or it may be that a particular exercise is not right for you. All these exercises must be performed smoothly through a full range of movement. When counting the tempo is controlled. Each move is –

lift and lower – 1 count

lift, lift, hold and lower – 2 counts

Exhale as you exert the effort, inhale as you relax. Above all enjoy yourself – smile and work those facial muscles at the same time!

19a Curl ups

Rectus abdominus

Lie down with the knees bent, feet flat on the floor. Place both hands behind the ears. Contract the stomach and curl the head and shoulders from the floor to feel the abdominals working. Be careful not to pull on the neck, let the head rest in the hands. Breathe out as you curl up. Keep the movement smooth and controlled. Rest as necessary. Do 2 sets of 8 repetitions.

19b Alternative curl up

Rectus abdominus

Lying down as above, alter the arm position by taking both arms above the head and hold onto both elbows pull the stomach in flat and slowly raise the head and shoulders to feel the abdominals working. Only come up as far as you can keeping the stomach flat. Remember to breathe out as you exert the effort, ie on the curl up. Do not pull on the head and neck. Do 2 sets of 8 repetitions.

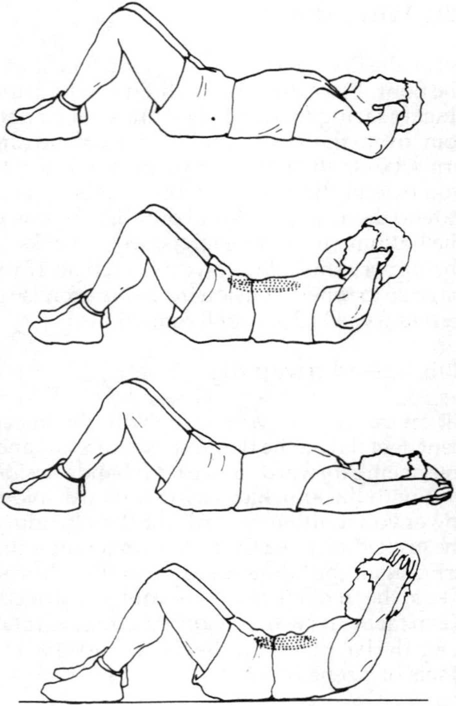

20a Tricep dip

Triceps

Sit on the floor with knees bent and feet flat on the floor. Place the hands behind you with the fingers facing forward. Now raise your bottom from the floor. Bend and extend the arms, be careful not to snap out the elbows as you extend the arms. Ensure you bend and extend the arms and do not only lift and lower the bottom. Feel this exercise in the backs of the upper arms. You can do stretch no 17 on page 26 to relieve tension from this exercise if necessary. Do 2 sets of 8 repetitions.

20b Raised tricep dip

Triceps

Sit on the edge of your chair with the knees bent, feet flat on the floor hip width apart and toes facing forward. Place both hands beside you with the knuckles facing forward. Now lower your bottom towards the floor bending the arms then raise the bottom extending the arms again but do not snap out the elbows. Keep the movement slow and controlled. Keep facing forwards. Contract stomach and keep the back straight. Rest as necessary. Do 2 sets of 8 repetitions.

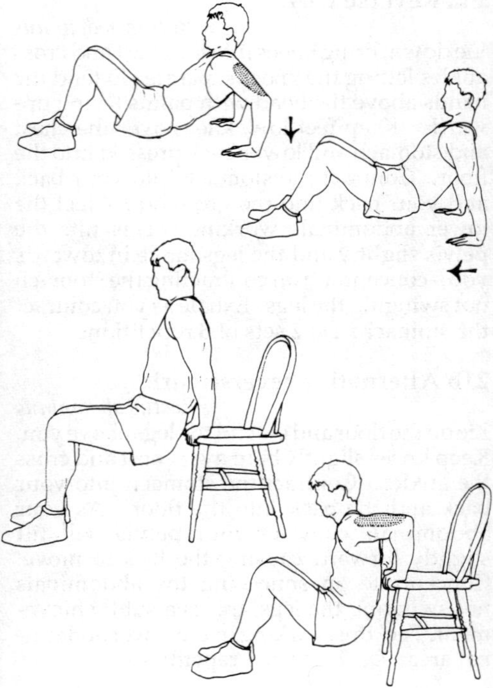

21a Reverse curl

Rectus abdominus

Lie down, bring knees into the chest and cross ankles letting the knees separate. Extend the hands above the head with palms facing upwards. Keep feet low, knees over the chest and stomach and lower back pressed into the floor. Contract the stomach into your back and your back into the ground and feel the lower abdominals working. This tilts the pelvis slightly and the legs move in towards you – concentrate on contracting the stomach not swinging the legs. Exhale as you contract the stomach. Do 2 sets of 8 repetitions.

21b Alternative reverse curl

Rectus abdominus

Lie on the floor and extend the legs above you. Keep knees slightly bent over chest and cross the ankles. Contract the stomach into your back and the back into the floor. As your abdominals contract your pelvis will tilt slightly forward causing the legs to move. Concentrate on squeezing the abdominals not swinging the legs, this is a subtle movement. Feel this working in the lower abdominal area. Do 2 sets of 8 repetitions

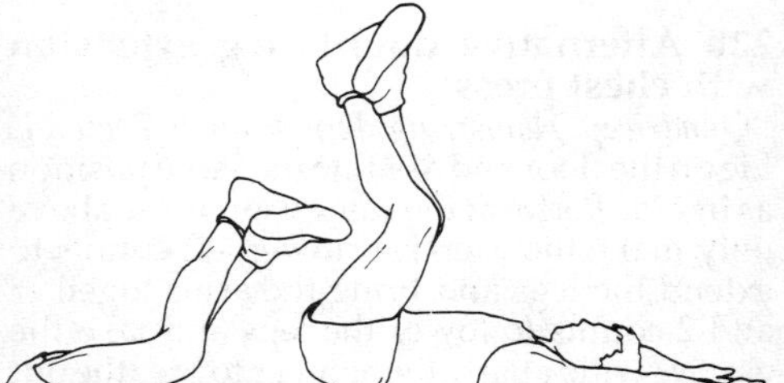

22a Double leg extension with chest press

Quadricep, Hamstring, Hip flexor & Pectorals

Lie on the floor with the knees raised over the body at a right angle. Push through the heels to extend the legs at the same time bringing the elbows and hands together in a chest press. As you bend the knees and lower the feet, take the elbows wide almost touching the floor and then repeat. Breathe out as you extend the legs. Keep the knees over the chest and the stomach pulled in flat to keep the lower back pressed down. Feel this exercise working the legs and the chest. Do 2 sets of 8 repetitions.

22b Alternative double leg extension with chest press

Quadricep, Hamstring, Hip flexor & Pectorals

Lie on the floor and assume the same position as in 22a. Perform the same exercise as above only make the exercise slower – 2 counts to extend the legs and bring the arms together and 2 counts to lower the legs and take the elbows wide apart. Remember to breathe out on the effort. Feel this exercise working the chest and legs. Do 2 sets of 8 repetitions.

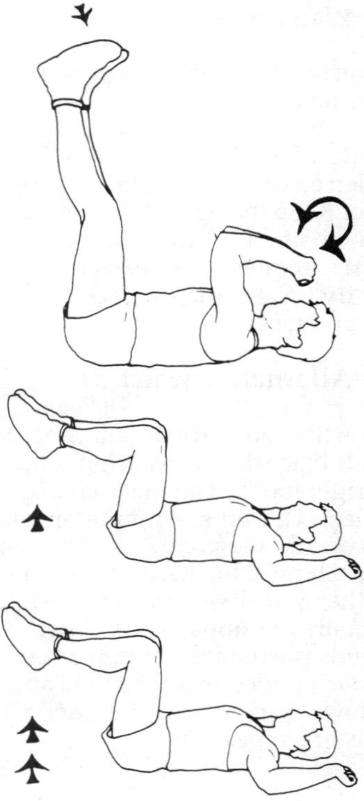

23a Waist twist

Obliques

Lie on the floor with the knees bent. Place the right ankle over the left knee. Place both hands behind the ears keeping the neck relaxed curl the shoulders off the floor and twist the left elbow and shoulder towards the right knee. Keep the right elbow on the floor to act as a pivot. Feel this exercise working the waist. Remember to exhale as you curl up and try to keep the stomach really flat. Do 2 sets of 8 repetitions.

23b Alternative waist twist

Obliques & Hip flexor

Lie on the floor with the knees bent hip width apart. Place the hands behind the ears. Keep the right foot flat on the floor and extend the left leg. The left knee simultaneously comes in towards the chest. As you contract the stomach raise the head and shoulders twisting the right elbow towards the left knee. As you curl the upper body down the left leg extends pushing through the heel. Keep the stomach pulled in all the time and do not let the lower back arch as you extend the leg. Do 2 sets of 8 repetitions.

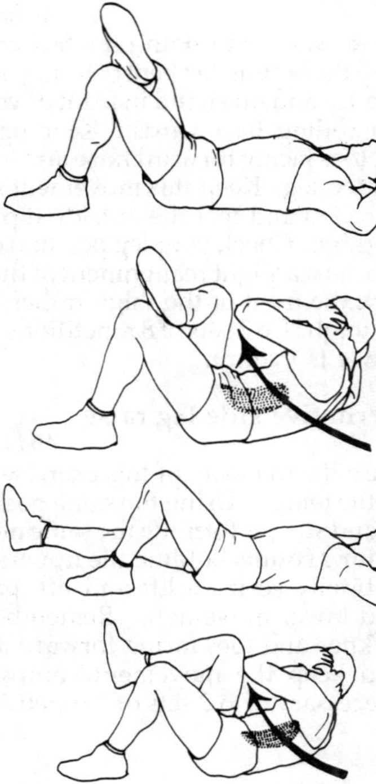

24a Side leg raises

Abductors

Lie on your side with both hips facing forward keep the bottom leg bent behind you for extra balance and one hand in front of you to stop you rolling backwards. Keeping the knee and toes facing forward raise and lower the extended leg. Keep this movement slow and controlled and feel the outside hip and thigh working. Check your leg position does not alter as just a slight realignment of the leg may work the front of the thigh rather than the outer thigh. Do 2 sets of 8 repetitions. Lift pause lower is 1 count.

24b Alternative side leg raise

Abductors

To increase the intensity of this exercise you can vary the tempo. Using the same position as above and still performing the same movement lift for 2 counts holding the uppermost position briefly so it's a lift and lift, pause lower and lower movement. Remember to keep the knee and toes facing forward at all times and keep the movement controlled. Rest as necessary. Do 2 sets of 8 repetitions.

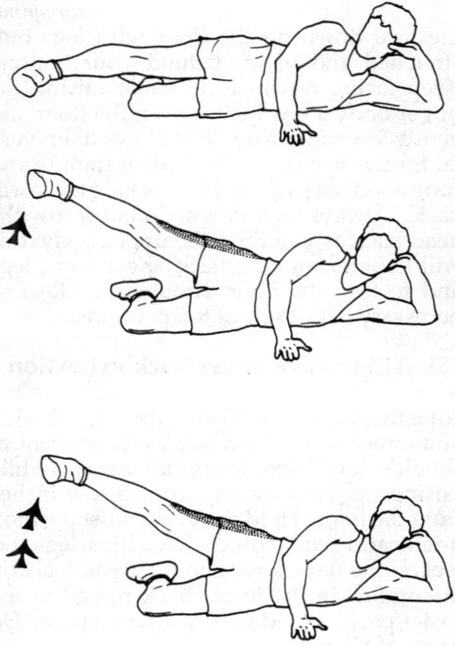

25a Lower back extension

Erector spinae

Lie face down on the floor with legs outstretched and hands behind your bottom. Keep facing downwards while raising the upper body a few inches from the floor and gently lowering. You do not have to lift very far for this to be effective, keep it smooth and controlled not jerky. Feel it working the lower back. Always look down, do not throw the head back as you raise the upper body, this will hyperextend the neck. Keep hips, legs and feet on the floor throughout. Rest as necessary. Do 2 sets of 8 repetitions.

25b Alternative lower back extension

Erector spinae

Alter the exercise by placing the hands beside you either side of the head, elbows bent at shoulder level. Keep facing downwards while raising upper body and arms a few inches from the floor. Hold the uppermost position briefly and gently lower. Keep hips, legs and feet on the floor throughout. If you feel any discomfort in the lower back return to the easier position and go at your own pace. Do 2 sets of 8 repetitions.

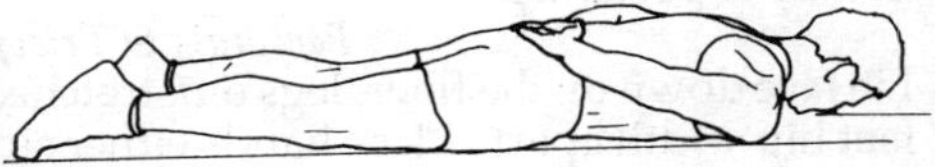

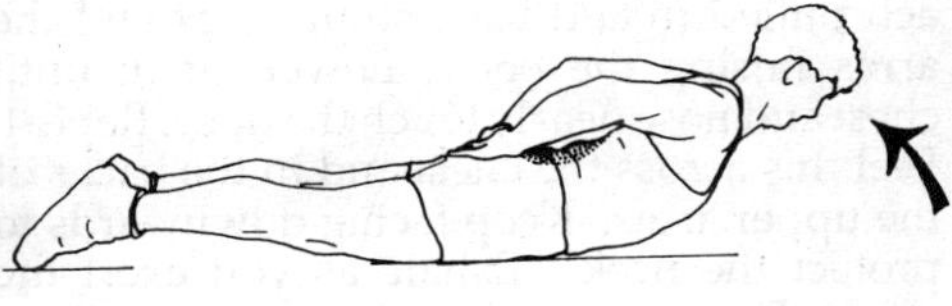

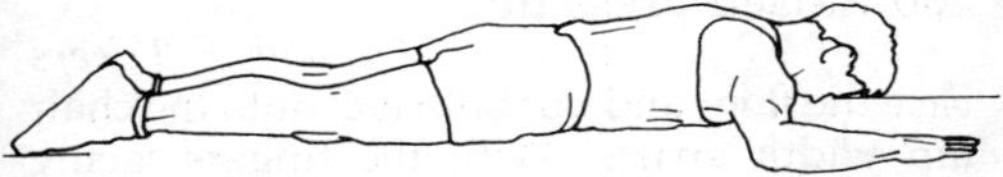

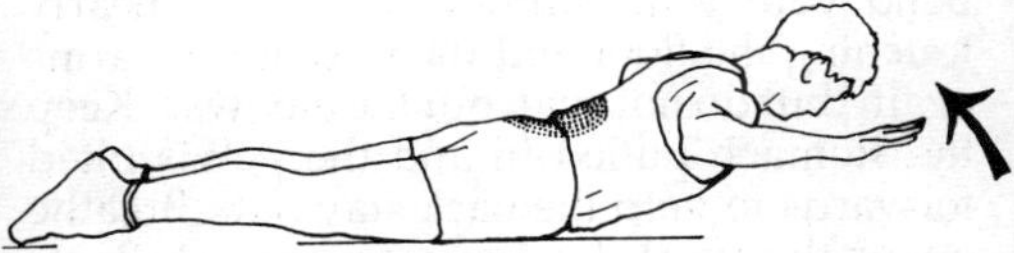

26a Full press up

Pectorals & Triceps

Lie face down on the floor, legs outstretched, feet hip width apart. Place hands either side of the head, shoulder width apart with arms bent and fingers facing forwards. With stomach pulled in and back straight, extend the arms raising the body. Lower again until chest and nose nearly touch the floor. Repeat. Feel this across the chest and in the backs of the upper arms. Keep facing downwards to protect the neck. Exhale as you exert the effort. Do 2 sets of 8 repetitions in your own time.

26b Raised press up

Pectorals & Triceps

Face the floor and put both feet onto the chair hip width apart. With the fingers facing forward and arms extended. Walk the hands out in front until the body is quite straight. Bend your arms until your nose is nearly touching the floor and then extend the arms again (but do not snap out the elbows). Keep the stomach pulled in and the pelvis tilted forwards to help the back stay flat. Breathe out on the effort. Rest as necessary. Do 2 sets of 8 repetitions in your own time.

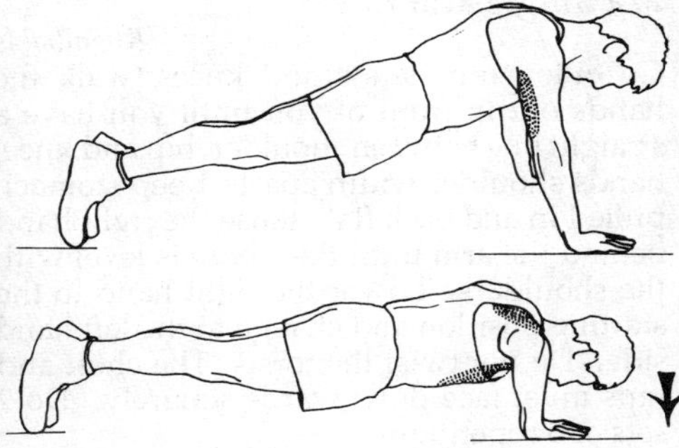

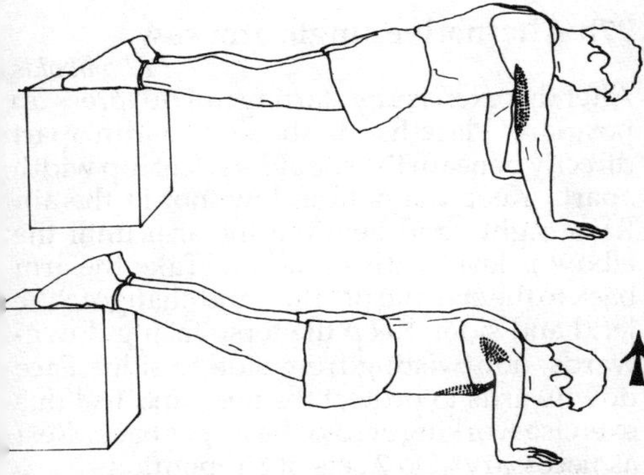

27a Single arm row

Rhomboids

Go onto your hands and knees, walk the hands out in front of you until you have a straight line between shoulder, hip and knee, hands shoulder width apart. Keep stomach pulled in and back flat. Raise the right hand behind the arm until the elbow is level with the shoulders. Lower the right hand to the starting position and change to the left hand side. Do not twist the torso. The chest and hips must face downwards squarely. Do 2 sets of 8 repetitions.

27b Alternative single arm row

Rhomboids

Alter this exercise by starting in a full press up position. Place hands shoulder width apart directly beneath the shoulders, feet hip width apart. Keep the bottom low, not in the air. Raise right hand bending the arm until the elbow is level with shoulder. Take the arm back to the starting position and change to the left hand side. Keep the torso facing downwards, not twisting from side to side. Face downwards to protect the neck and feel this exercise working across the upper back. Rest as necessary. Do 2 sets of 8 repetitions

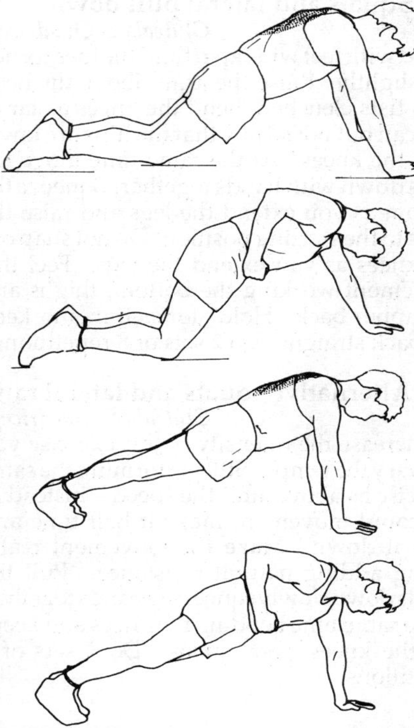

28a Squats and lateral pull down

Gluteals & Quadriceps

Stand with feet wide apart and the toes turned out slightly. Raise the arms above the head with fists clenched, bend the knees as far as you can but not so low that the hips are lower than the knees. At the same time move the arms down with hands together. Squeeze the bottom as you extend the legs and raise the arms to the starting position. Do not snap out the knees as you extend the legs. Feel this movement working the bottom, thighs and the upper back. Hold stomach in and keep the back straight. Do 2 sets of 8 repetitions.

28b Alternative squats and lateral raise

Gluteals & Quadriceps

To increase the intensity of this exercise you can vary the tempo. Still performing the same exercise as above alter the speed – instead of a 1 count movement make it half time and slow it down. Make the movement really strong adding natural resistance. Pull the hands down slowly squeezing hands together, at the same time bending the knees and keeping the knees over ankles. Do 3 sets of 8 repetitions.

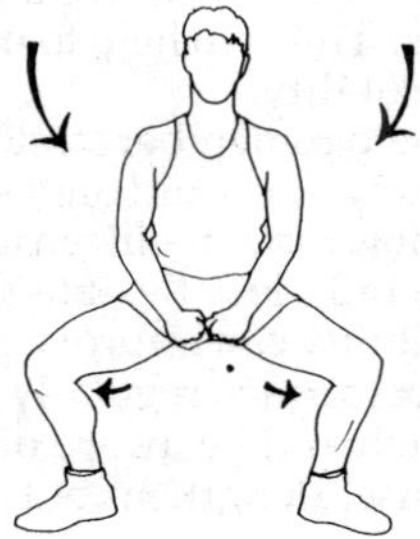

Cooldown

This is always the section that people think they can 'skip over' if they are running out of time. They often consider the 'real' exercises are over – this is *NOT* the case. It is equally important to stretch out after toning or aerobic exercises as it is to warm up before. These stretches prevent stiffness and soreness in the joints and muscles.

This time allows the body time to return to a pre-exercising state both mentally and physically. During exercise the muscles become shortened through repeatedly contracting them, but by performing some simple stretches they will return to their pre-exercising length. As the muscles are warmer after exercising you can hold the stretches for a little longer, 10-20 seconds. This will help to increase their range and flexibility.

It is important to remember stretching is very individual and you should only stretch as far as is comfortable for you – listen to your body. Men are generally less flexible than women but your flexibility can improve greatly if the stretches are performed regularly. You should hold the stretch and be aware of a mild tension as the muscle lengthens but it should not be painful. *Never bounce or force* a stretch position as this will evoke a *stretch reflex* which means the muscle automatically contracts to protect itself from being over stretched. If this occurs the muscle is unable to relax and lengthen properly. For the best results be patient and do the stretches regularly. You should always try to relax and breathe normally throughout this section and at the end you should feel relaxed and refreshed.

COOLDOWN STRETCHES

29 Standing quad stretch

Quadricep

Assume the correct posture check position. Bend the left supporting leg slightly. Draw the right heel in towards the bottom, holding the foot near the ankle, not curling the toes. Keep the hips parallel and the knees together. Feel the stretch in the front of the thigh. Push the hip forward to increase the stretch. Hold for 10-12 seconds, repeat on the other leg.

30 Standing calf stretch

Gastrocnemius

Assume the correct posture check position, place one heel behind you. The front leg is bent *(knee over ankle)* and the rear leg is straight, push through the back heel to the floor. Keep shoulders and hips parallel. Check the rear toe is facing forwards not out to the side as this can alter the muscle group you are aiming to stretch. Feel this stretch in the calf muscle in the rear leg. Hold for 10-12 seconds and repeat on the other side.

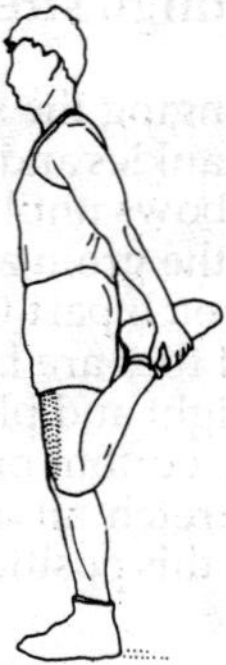

31 Seated inner thigh stretch

Adductors

Sit on the floor bringing the soles of the feet together. Hold the ankles and press the knees down with your elbows until you feel a comfortable stretch in the groin and inner thigh. To increase this stretch part the legs making sure the knees and toes are facing upwards. Keep the back straight and place your hands either behind your bottom or in front of the body. Feel this stretch all along the inner thigh. Do not force this position. Hold for 10-20 seconds.

32 Seated side stretch

Latissimus dorsi & Obliques

Sitting cross legged, place one hand slightly behind you on the floor, extend the other arm above you and reach over your head to feel a stretch all along the side of the body. Be careful not to roll sideways and do not lift the bottom off the floor. Hold for 10-12 seconds and repeat on the other side.

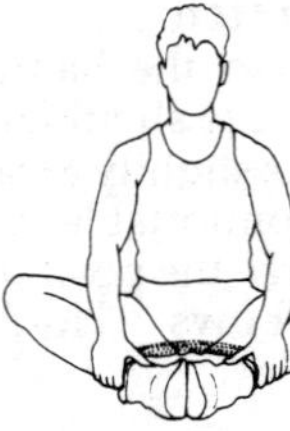

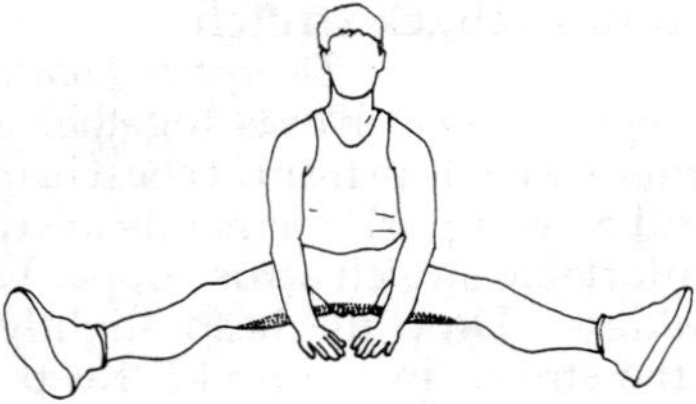

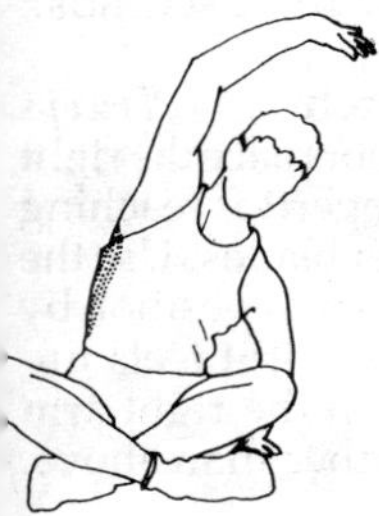

33 Seated chest stretch *Pectorals*

Sit cross legged, clasp the hands together behind you and squeeze shoulder blades together. Lift the hands slightly away from the back until you feel a comfortable stretch across the chest. Do not force the position, arch the back or lock out elbows. Hold for 10-12 seconds.

34 Seated upperback stretch *Deltoid & Trapezius*

Sit cross legged, clasp hands together and extend arms in a circle in front at chest height. Breathe out as you push the hands away to feel a comfortable stretch across upper back and shoulders. Drop the head slightly to increase the stretch in the neck. Keep the stomach pulled in. Hold for 10-12 seconds.

35 Seated upperarm stretch *Triceps*

Sitting cross legged on the floor place the right hand over your head with fingertips reaching down between your shoulder blades. Use the left hand to ease the right arm into position by holding onto the right elbow. If it feels uncomfortable then gently push the right arm from in front of the body rather than above. Hold for 10-12 seconds

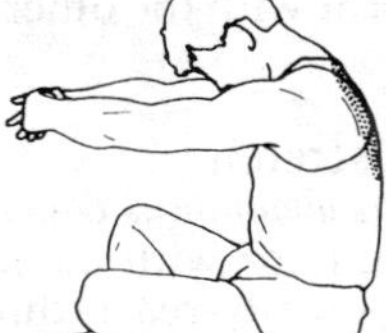

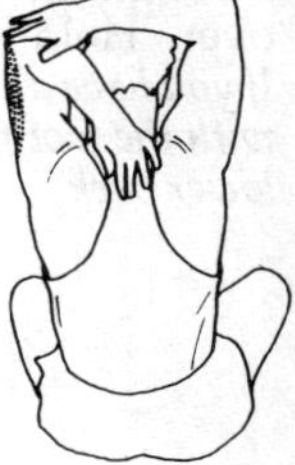

36 Back of thigh stretch

Hamstring

Lie on your back with knees bent, feet flat on the floor. Draw the right knee into the chest then gradually extend the leg supporting it by holding on behind the calf or thigh. The leg does not have to be straight just extend it until you feel a comfortable stretch behind the right thigh. Try to relax the upper body and breathe normally throughout. Hold for 10-20 seconds and repeat with the other leg.

37 Stomach stretch

Rectus abdominus & generally all over

Lie flat on the floor with the legs and arms outstretched – really reach through the fingertips and point your toes to feel a stretch throughout the stomach and generally all over. Hold for 10-12 seconds.

If you have any back problems keep one knee bent with the foot flat on the floor to help support the lower back.

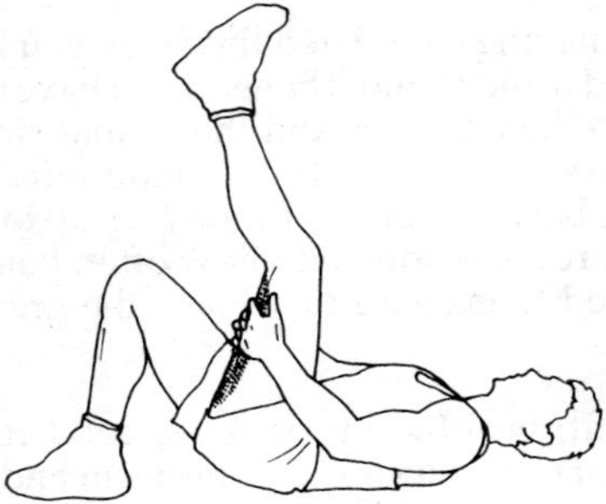

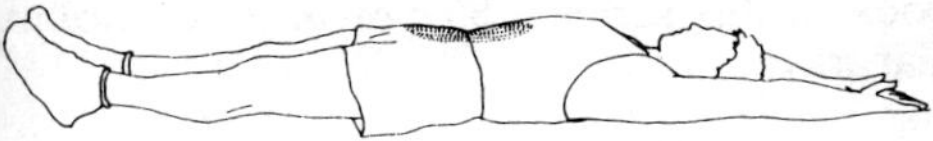

Summary

I hope having completed this book you have enjoyed it and found it beneficial. I have tried to keep the exercises and the format simple and easy to do whilst still being effective. Remember at the end of the day it's up to you how hard, how long and how often you are prepared to exercise to achieve the greatest results.

Being fit, healthy and looking good raises your self confidence and self esteem and can have a profound effect on your outlook towards life.

This book may only be a small step in achieving overall fitness but I hope you found it a significant one and will continue the exercises. You might find it fun to try another book in this series – *Step exercises* by Robin Gargrave.

Happy exercising!